The
UNITED
STATES
PRESIDENTS

Andrew JACKSON

Megan M. Gunderson

Big Buddy Books
An Imprint of Abdo Publishing
abdopublishing.com

abdopublishing.com

Published by Abdo Publishing, a division of ABDO, PO Box 398166, Minneapolis, Minnesota 55439.
Copyright © 2017 by Abdo Consulting Group, Inc. International copyrights reserved in all countries. No
part of this book may be reproduced in any form without written permission from the publisher. Big Buddy
Books™ is a trademark and logo of Abdo Publishing.

Printed in the United States of America, North Mankato, Minnesota
062016
092016

 THIS BOOK CONTAINS
RECYCLED MATERIALS

Design: Sarah DeYoung, Mighty Media, Inc.
Production: Mighty Media, Inc.
Editor: Lauren Kukla
Cover Photograph: Getty Images
Interior Photographs: Alamy (p. 19); AP Images (pp. 15, 21); Corbis (pp. 5, 7, 13, 17); Getty Images (p. 11);
    Library of Congress (pp. 7, 23, 25, 27, 29); North Wind (pp. 6, 9)

Cataloging-in-Publication Data

Names: Gunderson, Megan M., author.
Title: Andrew Jackson / by Megan M. Gunderson.
Description: Minneapolis, MN : Abdo Publishing, [2017] | Series: United States
    presidents | Includes bibliographical references and index.
Identifiers: LCCN 2015044079 | ISBN 9781680781014 (lib. bdg.) |
    ISBN 9781680775211 (ebook)
Subjects: LCSH: Jackson, Andrew, 1767-1845--Juvenile literature. 2. Presidents-
    -United States--Biography--Juvenile literature. | United States--Politics and
    Government--1829-1837--Juvenile literature.
Classification: DDC 973.5/6092092 [B]--dc23
LC record available at http://lccn.loc.gov/2015044079

Contents

Andrew Jackson

Andrew Jackson was the seventh US president. He was the first president to come from a poor family. Jackson later fought in the **War of 1812**. There, Jackson became a national hero. He soon became a leader in the **Democratic** Party.

In 1828, Jackson was elected president. While president, he fought for states' rights. He is remembered as a true **representative** of the people of the United States.

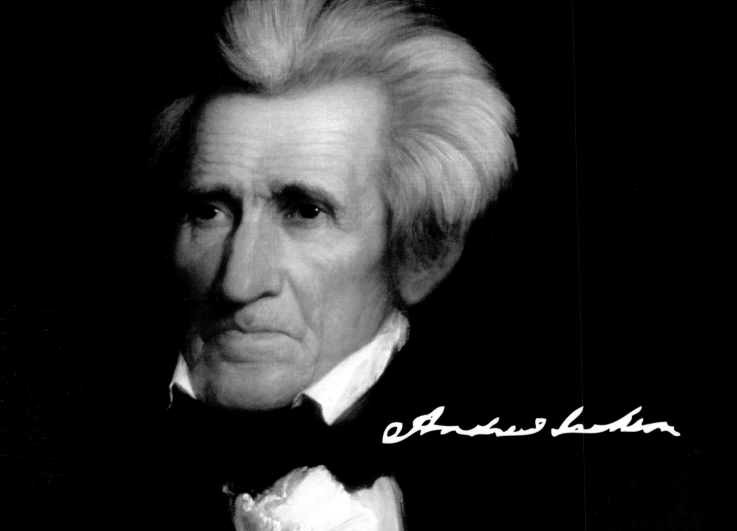

Timeline

1767
On March 15, Andrew Jackson was born in the Waxhaw settlement in South Carolina.

1821
President James Monroe appointed Jackson military governor of Florida.

1797
Jackson was elected to the US Senate.

1829
On March 4, Jackson became the seventh US president.

1832
Jackson was reelected president.

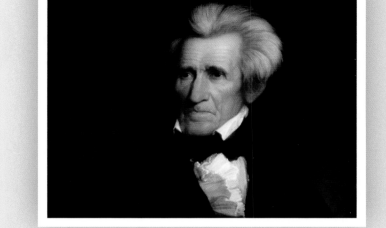

1830
Jackson signed the Indian Removal Act.

1845
On June 8, Andrew Jackson died.

7

Frontier Childhood

On March 15, 1767, Andrew Jackson was born in the Waxhaw settlement in South Carolina. Andrew's father died shortly before Andrew was born. Andrew had two older brothers, Hugh and Robert.

★ FAST FACTS ★

Born: March 15, 1767

Wife: Rachel Donelson Robards (1767–1828)

Children: none

Political Party: Democrat

Age at Inauguration: 61

Years Served: 1829–1837

Vice Presidents: John C. Calhoun, Martin Van Buren

Died: June 8, 1845, age 78

Andrew's birthplace was near the border of North Carolina and South Carolina.

Joining the Fight

The **American Revolution** reached the Waxhaw area in 1780. The same year, Andrew and Robert joined the **militia**. Then, in spring 1781, British soldiers captured Andrew, Robert, and other colonists.

While in prison, the brothers got sick. In time, they were rescued. But Robert died of his illness.

Andrew's mother, Elizabeth, nursed him back to health. However, she soon got sick and died. Andrew's brother Hugh had also died during the war. At age 14, Andrew was alone.

While captured, Andrew was attacked by a British officer. The attack scarred his head and arm.

Tennessee Lawyer

In 1784, Jackson went to Salisbury, North Carolina. There, he studied law. He worked very hard. In 1787, Jackson became a **lawyer**.

The following year, Jackson moved to Nashville. This region of North Carolina would soon be the new state of Tennessee. There, he began a successful law practice.

While in Nashville, Jackson met Rachel Donelson Robards. They were married in 1791. Five years later, Jackson bought a **plantation** near Nashville. He called it Hunter's Hill.

Jackson met Rachel when
he lived in a boardinghouse
owned by her family.

A New Leader

In 1796, Jackson began his **political** career. First, he helped write the Tennessee state **constitution**. Then, Jackson was elected to the US House of **Representatives**.

Jackson left Congress on March 4, 1797, and returned home. Later that year, he was elected to the US Senate. He served until 1798.

That same year, Jackson became a Tennessee **Supreme Court** judge. Jackson spent six years as a judge. Then he went back to work on his **plantation**.

In 1804, Jackson sold Hunter's Hill. He purchased this plantation, which he called the Hermitage.

The War of 1812

When the **War of 1812** began, Jackson joined the fight. At the time, many Native Americans were angry with the US government. US settlers were taking over their land. So, Native Americans fought with Great Britain against the United States.

During the war, Jackson led the Tennessee **militia**. In 1814, Jackson and his men won the Battle of Horseshoe Bend in Alabama. After the win, Jackson was put in charge of soldiers in Tennessee, Missouri, and Louisiana.

Jackson's men nicknamed their tough leader "Old Hickory." This is because hickory is one of the hardest, toughest kinds of wood.

War Hero

The **War of 1812** continued. Jackson was sent to guard the city of New Orleans, Louisiana. On January 8, 1815, Jackson won the Battle of New Orleans.

In 1821, President James Monroe made Jackson military governor of Florida territory. However, at the end of the year, Jackson stepped down.

Jackson then served on the US Senate for two years. Meanwhile, Jackson made a decision. He was going to run for president.

Nearly 2,000 British soldiers were hurt or killed in the Battle of New Orleans. The Americans lost just six men. This great victory made Jackson a war hero.

The 1824 election was unusual. Jackson earned 99 **electoral votes**. John Quincy Adams received 84. William H. Crawford received 41. Henry Clay won 37. No candidate had won a majority. So, there was no clear winner.

Clay decided to **support** Adams. So, Adams won the election. Then, Adams made Clay **secretary of state**. Jackson felt Clay had helped Adams so they could both get into office.

Jackson believed the voices of the American people had not been heard. He promised to fight for them. He started planning his next presidential campaign right away. Then, in 1828, Jackson won!

John C. Calhoun was elected Jackson's vice president.

President Jackson

Shortly after the election, something awful happened. Rachel Jackson died on December 22, 1828. Jackson was very sad.

Still, on March 4, 1829, Jackson was sworn in. He was the seventh US president. As president, Jackson often sought advice from outside his **cabinet**. This small group of friends became known as the Kitchen Cabinet.

★ DID YOU KNOW? ★

President Jackson is featured on the US $20 bill.

PRESIDENT JACKSON'S CABINET

First Term
March 4, 1829–March 4, 1833

★ **STATE:** Martin Van Buren,
Edward Livingston (from May 24, 1831)

★ **TREASURY:** Samuel D. Ingham,
Louis McLane (from August 8, 1831)

★ **WAR:** John H. Eaton,
Lewis Cass (from August 8, 1831)

★ **NAVY:** John Branch,
Levi Woodbury (from May 23, 1831)

★ **ATTORNEY GENERAL:** John M. Berrien,
Roger B. Taney (from July 20, 1831)

Second Term
March 4, 1833–March 4, 1837

★ **STATE:** Edward Livingston, Louis McLane (from
May 29, 1833), John Forsyth (from July 1, 1834)

★ **TREASURY:** Louis McLane, William J. Duane (from
June 1, 1833), Roger B. Taney (from September 23,
1833), Levi Woodbury (from July 1, 1834)

★ **WAR:** Lewis Cass

★ **NAVY:** Levi Woodbury,
Mahlon Dickerson (from June 30, 1834)

★ **ATTORNEY GENERAL:** Roger B. Taney,
Benjamin F. Butler (from November 18, 1833)

23

While Jackson was president, relations with Native Americans were **challenging**. The US government had promised land to Native Americans. But settlers moved onto the land.

Instead of keeping the government's promises, Jackson signed the Indian Removal Act of 1830. This forced all Native Americans to move west of the Mississippi River.

Meanwhile, South Carolina ignored a **tariff** meant to protect Northern

SUPREME COURT APPOINTMENTS

John Mclean: 1830

Henry Baldwin: 1830

James M. Wayne: 1835

Roger B. Taney: 1836

Philip P. Barbour: 1836

Jackson felt South
Carolina was abusing
its rights by ignoring
the federal government.

businesses. Jackson **supported** the **tariff**. But Vice President John C. Calhoun felt the tariff was unfair to the South. In 1832, Calhoun quit because of the disagreement.

While managing national issues, Jackson kept in mind his reelection. In 1832, Congress approved a bill to renew the national bank. Jackson felt the bank hurt businesses. So, he **vetoed** the bill.

Many voters agreed with Jackson's stand on the bank. He easily won the election. In 1833, he began his second term.

★ DID YOU KNOW? ★

Jackson vetoed more bills than any president before him.

Martin Van Buren was Jackson's secretary of state and then his vice president. From 1837 to 1841, Van Buren served as US president.

Final Years

President Jackson did not run for a third term. On March 4, 1837, Martin Van Buren became president. Jackson then returned home.

Jackson remained busy after his presidency. He watched over his **plantation**. He also stayed an active **Democrat**.

On June 8, 1845, Andrew Jackson died. He was buried at his plantation, next to Rachel. Jackson is remembered as a tough leader. He fought for what he felt was best for the American people.

Jackson's actions had an effect on politics for many years after his presidency.

Office of the President

Branches of Government

The US government has three branches. They are the executive, legislative, and judicial branches. Each branch has some power over the others. This is called a system of checks and balances.

★ Executive Branch

The executive branch enforces laws. It is made up of the president, the vice president, and the president's cabinet. The president represents the United States around the world. He or she also signs bills into law and leads the military.

★ Legislative Branch

The legislative branch makes laws, maintains the military, and regulates trade. It also has the power to declare war. This branch includes the Senate and the House of Representatives. Together, these two houses form Congress.

★ Judicial Branch

The judicial branch interprets laws. It is made up of district courts, courts of appeals, and the Supreme Court. District courts try cases. Sometimes people disagree with a trial's outcome. Then he or she may appeal. If a court of appeals supports the ruling, a person may appeal to the Supreme Court.

Qualifications for Office

To be president, a candidate must be at least 35 years old. The person must be a natural-born US citizen. He or she must also have lived in the United States for at least 14 years.

Electoral College

The US presidential election is an indirect election. Voters from each state choose electors. These electors represent their state in the Electoral College. Each elector has one electoral vote. Electors cast their vote for the candidate with the highest number of votes from people in their state. A candidate must receive the majority of Electoral College votes to win.

Term of Office

Each president may be elected to two four-year terms. The presidential election is held on the Tuesday after the first Monday in November. The president is sworn in on January 20 of the following year. At that time, he or she takes the oath of office.
It states:

> I do solemnly swear (or affirm) that I will faithfully execute the office of President of the United States, and will to the best of my ability, preserve, protect and defend the Constitution of the United States.

Line of Succession

The Presidential Succession Act of 1947 states who becomes president if the president cannot serve. The vice president is first in the line. Next are the Speaker of the House and the President Pro Tempore of the Senate. It may happen that none of these individuals is able to serve. Then the office falls to the president's cabinet members. They would take office in the order in which each department was created:

Secretary of State

Secretary of the Treasury

Secretary of Defense

Attorney General

Secretary of the Interior

Secretary of Agriculture

Secretary of Commerce

Secretary of Labor

Secretary of Health and Human Services

Secretary of Housing and Urban Development

Secretary of Transportation

Secretary of Energy

Secretary of Education

Secretary of Veterans Affairs

Secretary of Homeland Security

Benefits

★ While in office, the president receives a salary. It is $400,000 per year. He or she lives in the White House. The president also has 24-hour Secret Service protection.

★ The president may travel on a Boeing 747 jet. This special jet is called Air Force One. It can hold 70 passengers. It has kitchens, a dining room, sleeping areas, and more. Air Force One can fly halfway around the world before needing to refuel. It can even refuel in flight!

★ When the president travels by car, he or she uses Cadillac One. It is a Cadillac Deville that has been modified. The car has heavy armor and communications systems. The president may even take Cadillac One along when visiting other countries.

★ The president also travels on a helicopter. It is called Marine One. It may also be taken along when the president visits other countries.

★ Sometimes the president needs to get away with family and friends. Camp David is the official presidential retreat. It is located in Maryland. The US Navy maintains the retreat. The US Marine Corps keeps it secure. The camp offers swimming, tennis, golf, and hiking.

★ When the president leaves office, he or she receives lifetime Secret Service protection. He or she also receives a yearly pension of $203,700. The former president also receives money for office space, supplies, and staff.

PRESIDENTS AND THEIR TERMS

PRESIDENT	PARTY	TOOK OFFICE	LEFT OFFICE	TERMS SERVED	VICE PRESIDENT
George Washington	None	April 30, 1789	March 4, 1797	Two	John Adams
John Adams	Federalist	March 4, 1797	March 4, 1801	One	Thomas Jefferson
Thomas Jefferson	Democratic-Republican	March 4, 1801	March 4, 1809	Two	Aaron Burr, George Clinton
James Madison	Democratic-Republican	March 4, 1809	March 4, 1817	Two	George Clinton, Elbridge Gerry
James Monroe	Democratic-Republican	March 4, 1817	March 4, 1825	Two	Daniel D. Tompkins
John Quincy Adams	Democratic-Republican	March 4, 1825	March 4, 1829	One	John C. Calhoun
Andrew Jackson	Democrat	March 4, 1829	March 4, 1837	Two	John C. Calhoun, Martin Van Buren
Martin Van Buren	Democrat	March 4, 1837	March 4, 1841	One	Richard M. Johnson
William H. Harrison	Whig	March 4, 1841	April 4, 1841	Died During First Term	John Tyler
John Tyler	Whig	April 6, 1841	March 4, 1845	Completed Harrison's Term	Office Vacant
James K. Polk	Democrat	March 4, 1845	March 4, 1849	One	George M. Dallas
Zachary Taylor	Whig	March 5, 1849	July 9, 1850	Died During First Term	Millard Fillmore

PRESIDENT	PARTY	TOOK OFFICE	LEFT OFFICE	TERMS SERVED	VICE PRESIDENT
Millard Fillmore	Whig	July 10, 1850	March 4, 1853	Completed Taylor's Term	Office Vacant
Franklin Pierce	Democrat	March 4, 1853	March 4, 1857	One	William R.D. King
James Buchanan	Democrat	March 4, 1857	March 4, 1861	One	John C. Breckinridge
Abraham Lincoln	Republican	March 4, 1861	April 15, 1865	Served One Term, Died During Second Term	Hannibal Hamlin, Andrew Johnson
Andrew Johnson	Democrat	April 15, 1865	March 4, 1869	Completed Lincoln's Second Term	Office Vacant
Ulysses S. Grant	Republican	March 4, 1869	March 4, 1877	Two	Schuyler Colfax, Henry Wilson
Rutherford B. Hayes	Republican	March 3, 1877	March 4, 1881	One	William A. Wheeler
James A. Garfield	Republican	March 4, 1881	September 19, 1881	Died During First Term	Chester Arthur
Chester Arthur	Republican	September 20, 1881	March 4, 1885	Completed Garfield's Term	Office Vacant
Grover Cleveland	Democrat	March 4, 1885	March 4, 1889	One	Thomas A. Hendricks
Benjamin Harrison	Republican	March 4, 1889	March 4, 1893	One	Levi P. Morton
Grover Cleveland	Democrat	March 4, 1893	March 4, 1897	One	Adlai E. Stevenson
William McKinley	Republican	March 4, 1897	September 14, 1901	Served One Term, Died During Second Term	Garret A. Hobart, Theodore Roosevelt

35

PRESIDENT	PARTY	TOOK OFFICE	LEFT OFFICE	TERMS SERVED	VICE PRESIDENT
Theodore Roosevelt	Republican	September 14, 1901	March 4, 1909	Completed McKinley's Second Term, Served One Term	Office Vacant, Charles Fairbanks
William Taft	Republican	March 4, 1909	March 4, 1913	One	James S. Sherman
Woodrow Wilson	Democrat	March 4, 1913	March 4, 1921	Two	Thomas R. Marshall
Warren G. Harding	Republican	March 4, 1921	August 2, 1923	Died During First Term	Calvin Coolidge
Calvin Coolidge	Republican	August 3, 1923	March 4, 1929	Completed Harding's Term, Served One Term	Office Vacant, Charles Dawes
Herbert Hoover	Republican	March 4, 1929	March 4, 1933	One	Charles Curtis
Franklin D. Roosevelt	Democrat	March 4, 1933	April 12, 1945	Served Three Terms, Died During Fourth Term	John Nance Garner, Henry A. Wallace, Harry S. Truman
Harry S. Truman	Democrat	April 12, 1945	January 20, 1953	Completed Roosevelt's Fourth Term, Served One Term	Office Vacant, Alben Barkley
Dwight D. Eisenhower	Republican	January 20, 1953	January 20, 1961	Two	Richard Nixon
John F. Kennedy	Democrat	January 20, 1961	November 22, 1963	Died During First Term	Lyndon B. Johnson
Lyndon B. Johnson	Democrat	November 22, 1963	January 20, 1969	Completed Kennedy's Term, Served One Term	Office Vacant, Hubert H. Humphrey
Richard Nixon	Republican	January 20, 1969	August 9, 1974	Completed First Term, Resigned During Second Term	Spiro T. Agnew, Gerald Ford

PRESIDENT	PARTY	TOOK OFFICE	LEFT OFFICE	TERMS SERVED	VICE PRESIDENT
Gerald Ford	Republican	August 9, 1974	January 20, 1977	Completed Nixon's Second Term	Nelson A. Rockefeller
Jimmy Carter	Democrat	January 20, 1977	January 20, 1981	One	Walter Mondale
Ronald Reagan	Republican	January 20, 1981	January 20, 1989	Two	George H.W. Bush
George H.W. Bush	Republican	January 20, 1989	January 20, 1993	One	Dan Quayle
Bill Clinton	Democrat	January 20, 1993	January 20, 2001	Two	Al Gore
George W. Bush	Republican	January 20, 2001	January 20, 2009	Two	Dick Cheney
Barack Obama	Democrat	January 20, 2009	January 20, 2017	Two	Joe Biden

"It is to be regretted that the rich and powerful too often bend the acts of government to their selfish purpose." Andrew Jackson

★ WRITE TO THE PRESIDENT ★

You may write to the president at:
The White House
1600 Pennsylvania Avenue NW
Washington, DC 20500

You may e-mail the president at:
comments@whitehouse.gov

37

Glossary

American Revolution—the war between Americans and the British from 1775 to 1783. The Americans won their freedom from the British.

cabinet—a group of advisers chosen by the president to lead government departments.

challenge (CHA-luhnj)—something that tests one's strengths or abilities.

constitution (kahnt-stuh-TOO-shuhn)—the basic laws that govern a country or a state.

Democrat—a member of the Democratic political party.

electoral vote—a vote cast by a member of the Electoral College for the candidate who received the most popular votes in his or her state.

lawyer (LAW-yuhr)—a person who gives people advice on laws or represents them in court.

militia (muh-LIH-shuh)—people who help the army in times of need, they are not soldiers.

plantation—a large farm.

politics—the art or science of government. Something referring to politics is political. A person who is active in politics is a politician.

representative—someone chosen in an election to act or speak for the people who voted for him or her.

secretary of state—a member of the president's cabinet who handles relations with other countries.

support—to believe in or be in favor of something.

Supreme Court—the highest, most powerful court of a nation or a state.

tariff—the taxes a government puts on imported or exported goods.

veto—the right of one member of a decision-making group to stop an action by the group. In the US government, the president can veto bills passed by Congress. But Congress can override the president's veto if two-thirds of its members vote to do so.

War of 1812—a war between the United States and England from 1812 to 1815.

WEBSITES

★   ★

To learn more about the US Presidents, visit **booklinks.abdopublishing.com**. These links are routinely monitored and updated to provide the most current information available.

Index